MACEDONIA

THASOS

Mount Olympus

HELLESPONT

Troy

THESSALY

AEGEAN SEA

Thermopylae

Delphi
Thebes
ATTICA

GULF OF CORINTH
Eleusis
Marathon
Athens
Corinth
Piraeus
Miletus
Nemea
Salamis

Mycenae
DELOS

Olympia

N
W   E
S

Sparta

RHODES

[AFGHANISTAN]

N
EMPIRE
a
INDIA

THE PERSIAN EMPIRE IN 450 B.C.

ANCIENT GREECE

LIVING HISTORY

ANCIENT
GREECE

JOHN D. CLARE, Editor

GULLIVER BOOKS
HARCOURT BRACE & COMPANY
SAN DIEGO   NEW YORK   LONDON

HARCOURT BRACE

First published in Great Britain in 1993 by
The Bodley Head Children's Books

First U.S. Edition 1994

Library of Congress Cataloging-in-Publication Data
Ancient Greece/John D. Clare, editor. — 1st U.S. ed.
    p.   cm. — (Living history)
"Gulliver Books."
Includes index.
ISBN 0-15-200516-1
1. Greece — Civilization — To 146 B.C. — Juvenile literature.
2. Greece — History, Military — Juvenile literature. [1. Greece —
Civilization — To 146 B.C.] I. Clare, John D., 1952–
II. Series: Living history (San Diego, Calif.).
DF77.A585   1994
938 — dc20   93–6267

Printed and bound in China

A B C D E

Director of Photography	Tymn Lintell
Photography	Charles Best
Art Director	Dalia Hartman
Production Manager, Photography	Fiona Nicholson
Typesetting	Thompson Type, San Diego, California
Reproduction	Scantrans, Singapore

ACKNOWLEDGMENTS

Historical Advisor: Michael Edwards, University of London. **Casting:**
Baba's Crew (UK), Jenny Panoutsopoulou (Greece). **Costumes:** Val
Metheringham, Angi Woodcock. **Locations, Greece:** Susan Pugh-
Tasios, Pat Arvaniti. **Makeup:** Emma Scott. **Props:** Cluny South,
Marisa Rossi. **Runners:** Zoë Pagnamenta (Greece and UK), Catherine
Stroobants (Greece). **Sets and transport:** Road Runner Film Services
and Peter Knight. **Maps and timeline:** John Laing. **Map and timeline
illustrations:** David Wire.

Additional photographs: American School of Classical Studies at
Athens: Agora Excavations, p. 27 bottom left, p. 63 left. Ancient Art &
Architecture Collection, p. 10, p. 16 middle left, top right. Ashmolean
Museum, p. 45 middle, p. 51 top right. Bildarchiv Preussischer
Kulturbesitz, Berlin, p. 21. British Museum, p. 6 left, p. 16 bottom left,
p. 27 top and right, p. 41 top, p. 45 left and right. Ecole Française
d'Archéologie, Athens, p. 63 top. Kevin Fleming/Ulysses Archive,
pp. 18–19. Hellenic Navy, pp. 28–29. Michael Holford, p. 11, p. 12, p. 14,
p. 52, p. 57, p. 62 left and bottom. Metropolitan Museum of Art:
Fletcher Fund, 1932 (32.11.1), photograph Schecter Lee, p. 30 left;
Rogers Fund, 1914 (14.130.120) p. 17. Museum of Fine Arts, Boston,
H. L. Pierce Fund, p. 9. Luciano Pedicini, p. 28, p. 35, pp. 54–55.
Royal Ontario Museum, Toronto, p. 13, p. 31 bottom. Scala, p. 6 right,
p. 7, p. 31 top. Staatlichen Antikensammlungen und Glyptothek,
Munich, photograph Studio Koppermann, p. 30 bottom.

Contents

The Greek World

The philosopher Socrates (*c.* 470–399 B.C.) lived in Athens, the most splendid city in ancient Greece. Scholars have called him "the wisest man of his time," but he never heard of the American continents, or electricity, or germs. People

in his city could buy and sell other people as slaves, and to punish a wrongdoer they might cut off his or her hand. In many ways ancient Greek society may seem primitive and unsophisticated to modern people. Yet in the centuries after 500 B.C., Greek ideas changed the world — and now, 2,500 years later, many of our ideas about government and culture can be traced back to ancient Greek ways of thinking and living.

Many modern states are democracies; they believe in the principle of rule "by the people for the people." The Greeks were the first to develop this form of government, allowing men (though not women) who met certain requirements to vote for officials and laws.

Ancient Greece also produced a number of influential philosophers who asked important questions and tried to organize thoughts about life, people, and the universe. The works of Greek philosophers such as Socrates, Plato (*c.* 428–348 B.C.), and Aristotle (384–322 B.C.) are still studied today, and Greek ideas are the foundation of modern thinking about science, medicine, mathematics, and geography.

The Greeks' artistic achievements were equally significant. Many Western ideas about sculpture and architecture originated in their elegant statues and buildings. The Greeks especially prized drama and the theater. In huge outdoor amphitheaters, men, women, and children gathered to see tragedies by Aeschylus (525–456 B.C.) or Euripides (*c.* 484–406 B.C.), or comedies

by Aristophanes (*c.* 450–388 B.C.). The Greeks' plays have inspired authors and audiences in every century since they were written.

The ancient Greeks even influenced the way we think of competitive sports. The modern Olympic Games are based on contests held every four years in Greece, and English words such as "athletics," "stadium," and "marathon" all come from Greek.

THE FIRST GREEKS

The Greeks were not the first people to establish a civilization in the land we know as Greece. On Crete, a large Greek island, archaeologists have found the ruins of rich palaces dating from about 2000 B.C. They belonged to a people called the Minoans. In about 1600 B.C. a similar civilization developed at Mycenae on the mainland, but Mycenae was destroyed in about 1200 B.C.

Historians think that the next 400 years were a "Dark Age" of wars, invasions, and movements of tribes. Nobody really knows where the first Greeks came from, but many historians think they developed from a number of different tribes that came to Greece from India and central Europe during these years. In a book titled *Black Athena,* the historian Martin Bernal claims that the Greeks came from Egypt and Africa. Whatever their origin, after about 800 B.C. Greek civilization began to take form.

THE CITY-STATES

Around this time, the Greeks began to think of themselves as one people, the Hellenes (it was the Romans who, later, named them Greeks). They despised most foreigners, calling them barbarians — because foreign languages made a ridiculous sound like *bar-bar* to Greek ears. Still, Greece was not a single, unified country. The mainland is divided by rocky mountain ranges, and the Gulf of Corinth cuts southern Greece off from the north. Many small islands dot the Aegean Sea. Perhaps because of these natural barriers, ancient Greece was divided into dozens of tiny states, each consisting of a city and the nearby farmland. Athens was the largest of these city-states; Sparta, Corinth, and Thebes were also important. The

other city-states were much smaller. They were all continually at war, trying to gain dominance over each other.

Different city-states had different forms of government. Most were controlled by a small group of rich landowners and noblemen. Some, such as Athens, were democracies. In others, a tyrant seized power and ruled by himself. Sparta, unlike any other *polis* (city), was governed by two kings, who were advised by a council of men over 60 years old.

Class was important to all Greeks. Only aristocrats were considered fit to govern, and even in a democracy only certain men, known as citizens, were allowed to own land or to vote. Athenian women could claim a kind of citizenship, though they could not own land or vote; according to a law passed in 451 B.C., a woman had to come from parents who were both Athenian in order to entitle her children to citizenship. *Metoikoi* (barbarians and Greeks from other cities) might be quite wealthy, but they could not own land or buildings, and they were kept from voting. Slaves were at the bottom of the social scale; some were officially owned by the city-state and could be lent to various landowners as city officials saw fit.

Far left: *A statue of the Athenian philosopher Socrates.*
Left: *A mosaic of two masks for actors.*
Above: *A Greek painting shows two Amazons, mythical women warriors, attacking a Greek soldier.*

Farming in Attica

With a population of perhaps 250,000 people, Athens was the largest and most populated city-state in Greece in 431 B.C. The countryside around Athens was called Attica; another 250,000 people lived there. Townspeople joked that country folk were slow and stupid, but it was country folk who provided food for the many city dwellers.

Attica was a hilly region, and the soil there was full of rocks. There was little rain. Plato wrote that Attica was like "the skeleton of a body withered by disease — the soil has fallen away, leaving the land all skin and bone."

Though landowning farmers had the privileges of citizenship, not all of them enjoyed the privileges of wealth. Farming was hard work. In winter the cold north winds would "skin an ox," and in summer "the sun scorches head and knees," wrote Hesiod, an eighth-century farmer and poet. Wealthy estate owners, who kept slaves, horses, and oxen to work their fields, could afford large farmhouses and homes in town. Poor farmers, however, were forced to rely on their own strength and had "for robe but a rag, for bed just a bag of rushes — the home of a nation of bugs whose fierce and

tireless bites keep you awake at night."

But after the harvest, wrote Hesiod, country life was wonderful — even for the lowliest farmer: "The grasshopper sings, and the goats are fattest and the women most beautiful. . . . Then I'll have a shady rock and bright wine, a bowl of curds, some goat's milk, and a nice piece of veal."

A farmer loads his donkey with eggs, chickens, cheese, and vegetables to sell in the marketplace in Athens. From the branches of the farmer's olive trees, cheeses not yet ready for market hang in linen bags to strain out the whey (water). While the farmer prepares for market with the help of his wife, his daughters make bread and his son milks one of the family's goats — cows' milk is thought to be too rich for Greek stomachs. Against the farmhouse

rest a plow, several sickles that will be used to reap the barley crop, and other farming tools.
Above: *Athenian farmers grow mainly olives, which do well even without much rain. Here a farmer adds his weight to that of a bag of rocks on an olive press to help squeeze oil out of the olives. Olive oil is used for cooking, in lamps, and to remove dirt from the body.*

Sparta

For a long time Spartans, who placed a tremendous emphasis on physical strength and military prowess, had the strongest army in Greece. They enslaved inhabitants of neighboring areas and forced them to do all the city-state's farming and trading. This allowed the Spartan men to spend all their time training to be fierce warriors. Sparta was constantly vying with other city-states for power, and Athens was its greatest rival. Nonetheless, the army was so strong that no city walls encircled Sparta; its soldiers were considered protection enough.

Spartan children belonged to the state, not to their parents. The elders inspected all newborn babies; those thought to be weak were left on the hills to die.

For his first few years, a Spartan boy lived with his mother. At 7, he went to live in army barracks, to be trained by a *paidonomos* (ruler of children). Boys had no other education. Spartan men always ate together in their barracks. The young men ate in silence, lowering their eyes to demonstrate re-

spect for their elders. Their meals usually consisted of barley bread, fruit, cheese, and a black broth. Although a young man usually married when he was 20, he had to live ten more years in the barracks, slipping away secretly at night to visit his wife.

Spartan men were not allowed to show pain or weakness. In one story a youth who had stolen a fox and hidden it in his shirt was on his way back to the barracks when an older man stopped him. Because Spartan children had to show respect for their elders, the boy talked to the man and ignored the fox, which was biting his chest and stomach. When he returned to the barracks he died of his wounds — but had never flinched.

Spartan boys spend time away from the city training. They have no shoes and wear only a thin tunic, even in winter. They are encouraged to steal food but are whipped if they are caught.
Left: *Spartan girls are trained in athletics, so they will grow strong and bear strong children; they wear so little that Greeks from other city-states are shocked. Unlike their brothers, Spartan girls live at home.*
Above: *Spartan men boxing; they wear* kimantes — *gloves made of ox-hide thongs tied around their hands.*

Gods, Goddesses, and Heroes

The Greeks worshiped many gods and goddesses, all of whom had human characteristics and emotions; they could fall in love, fight, or weep. Most were said to live on Mount Olympus, in northern Greece.

The king of the immortals was Zeus, god of thunder and lightning; he had married one of his sisters, a jealous goddess named Hera, whom the Greeks feared. Two of Zeus's brothers were also rulers: Poseidon, god of the sea; and Hades, lord of the dead, who lived in the underworld. Another of Zeus's sisters, Demeter, was mankind's best friend, goddess of the harvest. Zeus's son Apollo was the god of light and purity, music and healing; his daughter Athene was the goddess of war, handicrafts, and wisdom, and the patron deity of Athens.

Aphrodite, who sprang from the foam on the sea, was the goddess of love. Dionysus, the god of wine, acting, and destruction, was a favorite of the Greeks.

Greek myths, or stories about the gods and goddesses, are full of conflict and violence. One myth concerns Typhon, a fierce monster with dragon's wings and 100 heads, each with a mouth roaring, howling, and shouting in a different voice. The Greeks said Zeus defeated Typhon by throwing the island of Sicily on top of him. This story helped explain why the volcanic Mount Etna in Sicily occasionally erupted — Typhon was trying to escape.

Where do we come from? The myths said that the god Prometheus made people from clay, then stole fire from the gods and gave it to mankind.

The Greeks believed that the gods and goddesses were not only powerful but also jealous; they could make trouble if dis-

pleased. This explained pain, disease, and disaster. According to one story, when the gods gave Athens to Athene, Poseidon was so angry that he sent a huge tidal wave to flood the land.

THE HEROES

The Greeks also told many stories about human heroes; some of these may have been based on actual events in the distant past.

The greatest hero was Heracles (Hercules) of Thebes, celebrated all over Greece for his strength. In one story he completes a number of labors, or tasks, including overcoming animals such as the enormous lion of Nemea and the fierce bull of King Minos.

Theseus, the mythic hero most admired in Athens, was intelligent and kind, as well as brave and strong. He killed the Mino-taur — a monster with the head of a bull and the body of a man, the offspring of the bull Heracles defeated — and became the ruler of Athens.

The Greek poet Homer, who probably lived in the ninth or eighth century B.C., made the story of the siege of Troy, a city in Asia Minor (present-day Turkey), famous in the epic poem the *Iliad*. The *Iliad* may describe actual raids on the city; archaeologists have found evidence that Troy was attacked and burned a number of times. Homer's other great epic, the *Odyssey*, describes how the hero Odysseus returned home from Troy.

Left: The Athenians believe that "gray-eyed" Athene, who gave olives and women to men, was born fully grown and dressed in armor when Hephaistos, the black-smith god, split Zeus's head open with an ax.
Right: The statue of Athene in the Parthenon temple in Athens stands 40 feet (12 meters) high and is plated with over a ton (1,000 kilograms) of gold.

13

Sacrifices and Festivals

The Greeks believed that although the gods and goddesses were far away, their blessing or curse could bring instant success or disaster. Many people, therefore, were very superstitious. If they heard the howling of an owl, the bird sacred to Athene, they shouted, "Athene is queen!" If a sacred breed of snake slithered through their house, they built a shrine on the spot.

The best way to please a god or goddess was to offer a sacrifice, usually a sheep or pig. Such a ceremony, which could take place in a home or by a temple, was common, and poor people often clubbed together to buy an animal between them. The whole family joined in the sacrifice, laying their hands on the animal while the head of the household, standing upright with his arms raised, prayed to the gods for health and wealth. They threw barley over the animal, slit its throat, burned its thigh bones, and finally cooked and ate the meat.

At festivals, which could last several days, many sacrifices were offered. All the inhabitants of Athens took part in the festival of Panathenaea (the Greek word *pan* means "all"). The people sang as they marched through the city, "Athene, our city's protector, queen of a land powerful in war, come to us bringing victory."

Many festivals were farming ceremonies. Perhaps most important of these was the festival of the Eleusinian Mysteries, celebrated in Athens during late summer. People came from all over to Greece to honor Demeter, goddess of the harvest, by taking part in the 21 days of festivities.

The Greeks believed that their gods and goddesses watched these festivals. To amuse them, they put on athletic contests and races in which the runners carried burning torches; they also held acting, public speaking, and choral singing competitions.

To seek advice from the gods, Greeks go to one of the 250 oracles in Greece. People who seek Apollo's advice travel to Delphi, wash themselves, and sacrifice an animal on the altar outside the Temple of Apollo. Then they go to the Adyton — the holy of holies, or most sacred spot — located inside the temple. Below the Adyton lies a cavern through which a sacred stream flows. In the cavern, a priestess called the Pythoness is in a drugged frenzy brought on by inhaling fumes from the stream and chewing laurel leaves; in her babbling and shouting there will be a message from Apollo. A priest listens to her; later he will interpret the message for the visitors, phrasing it in the form of a riddle.

Left: *A vase painting shows the goddess Demeter sending a messenger to Greece with the gift of wheat.*

The Olympic Games

First held in 776 B.C., the Olympic Games in honor of Zeus took place every four years in the city of Olympia in southern Greece. The games were a major religious festival, and in 388 B.C. the orator (speaker) Lysias claimed that "they bring us together and create peace and understanding among us."

The festival lasted for five days in summer. A month-long sacred truce, during which war between city-states stopped, allowed 20,000 priests, competitors, and spectators to travel from all over Greece to the games. Most visitors slept in tents, but in later times important guests stayed in a huge building called the Leonidaion. A large marble temple containing a gold-and-ivory statue of Zeus was known as one of the seven wonders of the ancient world.

The Olympics started with prayers and religious ceremonies, then the games themselves began. Competitions included boxing, horse racing, and a pentathlon of five events: a 200-yard (180-meter) sprint race, javelin and discus throwing, long jumping, and wrestling. In another wrestling competition, called the *pankration,* the fighters were allowed to do anything apart from biting an opponent or gouging out his eye. The judge carried a stick and hit anybody who cheated. There were also competitions in public speaking and poetry.

Winners at Olympia became celebrities. In 415 B.C. one Athenian, Alcibiades, was appointed general of a military expedition because he had entered seven chariots in one race in the Olympic Games and had won first, second, and fourth places. In Sparta, Olympic winners had the honor of fighting in the front rank during the next war.

Olympic athletes like these runners (right) and horseback riders (left, below) compete naked.
Left, above: *Every athlete longs for the victor's ribbon. Although his prize is a simple laurel wreath, when he returns home he will be loaded with presents. In some cities he will be freed from paying taxes; in others he may be given free meals for the rest of his life.*
Above: *Two athletes are wrestling while a javelin thrower tests the point of his javelin. To the left is an athlete in the usual starting position for a race. The sprint race takes place on the third day of the games. After the race, an ox is sacrificed to Zeus and the winner is allowed to set fire to the sacrifice.*

The Greek Colonies

As Greek civilization developed, so did the Greeks' desire to spread their culture and influence to other lands. In about 800 B.C., the Hellenes started to sail to other countries to set up colonies, a process that was to last for eight centuries.

Greek governments convinced people to move to the colonies for a number of reasons. Sometimes when the population of a city had outgrown the amount of food that could be produced on the surrounding farmland, starting a colony offered a way to increase production. In such cases a respected local man was appointed as "founder," to lead the expedition. Sometimes a section of the population that was being badly treated would decide to emigrate, hoping to find a better life. In other cases, a whole city at war with a powerful neighbor might pack up and sail to a safer place.

The first colonies were set up in Sicily, Italy, and Asia Minor. Some groups went as far afield as Massilia (Marseilles) in southern France, Naucratis in Egypt, and Olbia (near the Crimea) on the Black Sea. One historian has estimated that there were 150 city-states in Greece itself but 1,500 colonies around the Mediterranean and Black seas. Most colonies copied the culture and government of the city-state that had founded them, and many eventually became centers of Greek civilization and learning.

Greek colonists sail on a merchant ship.
Above: *The map shows the main Greek settlements around the Mediterranean and Black seas in about 500 B.C.*

Marathon

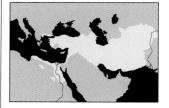

The spread of Greek colonies brought Greece to the attention of the great Persian Empire. In 492 B.C. the Persian king, Darius, sent ambassadors to the Greeks, demanding that they accept him as their master. "If you want Greek land and water, help yourselves," the Greeks replied as they threw the ambassadors into deep pits.

Two years later, Darius sent a large army to conquer Greece. His fleet crossed the Aegean Sea and landed at Marathon Bay, 20 miles (32 kilometers) north of Athens. Greek writers of the time claimed that the Persians had 100,000 men while the Athenian army was only about 9,000 strong.

These numbers were probably exaggerated, but the Athenians were outnumbered.

The Athenian general Miltiades ordered an Olympic athlete named Pheidippides to run the 125 miles (200 kilometers) to Sparta to ask for help. "You have won the laurel wreath at Olympia. Now win glory for Athens!" Miltiades commanded. Stopping only once, Pheidippides reached Sparta in two days. The Spartans, however, refused to join the Athenians until the full moon, in five days' time. Pheidippides ran back to Marathon with the bad news. The entire mission had taken only four days.

Miltiades then placed the strongest soldiers on the wings (the outer sides) of his army and ordered his men to charge the Persians. Although the center of the Athenian army gave way, the two wings broke through the Persian lines and turned back to surround the Persians, who panicked and fled.

Above: *Pheidippides runs to Sparta.*
Far left: *One of Darius's soldiers ready for battle.*
Left: *The Persian Empire c. 490 B.C.*
Below: *This soldier is having trouble dressing his friend's wound because he has wound both ends of the bandage around the same way.*

Thermopylae and Salamis

In 480 B.C. Darius's son Xerxes set sail for Greece with, one writer claimed, 5 million men and 1,200 ships. Such figures are impossible, but even so Xerxes was so confident that when some Greek spies were captured he showed them his army and set them free to make their report.

Alarmed by the strength of the Persian army, 31 Greek city-states, including Athens and Sparta, formed an alliance. An army of 7,000 soldiers commanded by Leonidas, one of the Spartan kings, went north to Thermopylae, a narrow strip of land between the mountains and the sea; the Greeks hoped to halt Xerxes there.

A traitor, however, showed the Persians a secret pass through the hills, allowing them to sneak up on the Greeks. As the alarm was sounded, most of the Greeks retreated. Leonidas and 300 men stayed; they fought to the death, delaying Xerxes' advance.

Next the Persian army marched on Athens. The city's women and children had fled south, so it was almost deserted. The Persians defeated the few defenders and burned Athens to the ground.

But the Athenians still had their navy. Together with warships from other city-states, this fleet lay west of the city, in the Straits of Salamis. In a fierce battle, the Persian fleet was destroyed. As a result, Xerxes was forced to go home. Greece had survived.

A Greek trireme (a galley with three banks of oars) rams a Persian ship at the Battle of Salamis. The Greek fleet includes 310 triremes; each is commanded by a man under the age of 50 and has a crew of 4 archers; 10 marines, ages 20 to 30; and 170 rowers.

Half the Greek navy lures the Persian fleet into battle in the narrow straits, where a strong breeze makes it difficult to move freely. The other half then surprises them by attacking from the rear. The Persian ships are smaller and more maneuverable, but the heavier Greek ships are able to ram and sink them.

Silver and Grain

Why did Xerxes, ruler of an empire that stretched 3,000 miles (5,000 kilometers) from Asia Minor to India, fail to conquer the Greek city-states? Greek historians claimed that Xerxes' pride combined with the Greek warriors' bravery to cause his downfall; they ignored the difficulties he faced by fighting far from home. Since Xerxes' capital, Susa, was a three-months journey away from Athens, it is remarkable that he could mount an invasion at all.

Also important was Greece's growing economic strength. When Xerxes invaded, Athens in particular was thriving; the powerful Athenian fleet had been financed with profits from a rich vein of silver discovered in southern Attica in 483 B.C., just before the Persians invaded. Athens was also growing rich as a center of trade, with *metoikoi* merchants trading in all sorts of goods, from Egyptian rigging, sails, and papyrus to African ivory. The most important trade was in grain, since the farms of Attica could never have fed the population of Athens. In 335 B.C. a Greek writer claimed that the Crimea alone sent 17,000 tons of wheat a year to Athens.

Left: *A scribe lists Athens's imports.*
Opposite page: *Leather from Sicily; a silver coffeepot from Asia Minor; tin from Britain; dyes from Syria; grain from Sicily, Cyrene, Egypt, and the Black Sea; French wine; Hellespont mackerel; copper from Cyprus; ivory and cloth from Africa; and wood from Macedon.*
This page: *To pay for these imports, Athens exports (above) jewelry, pottery, olives, and grapes.*

Athenian Democracy

Athens was a democracy, a state ruled by its citizens. It was not, however, like a modern democracy, under which the people elect lawmakers to make decisions in a congress or parliament; in Athens, male landowners who qualified for citizenship decided for themselves such matters as whether to go to war or put unsuccessful generals to death. They met on a hill in Athens called the Pnyx, where they voted by a show of hands. Women, slaves, and the *metoikoi* could not be full citizens and had no say in the government.

The citizens' assembly, the *ekklesia*, met from 30 to 40 times a year. It was supposed to meet early in the day, and every citizen over 20 years old was supposed to attend. In practice, however, perhaps only one-tenth of the citizens attended regularly, and one writer complained that when he arrived on time he was the only one there. It was often noon before everyone had assembled.

The meeting started with the sacrifice of a black pig, followed by prayers. If rain began to fall, it was a bad omen and the meeting was canceled. Everybody had the right to speak, and the crowd interrupted and yelled abuse whenever they disagreed. If you supported a speaker, you called him a *rhetor* (orator); if you opposed him, you referred to him as a *demagogue* (mob leader). The historian Thucydides (*c.* 460–399 B.C.) described how such a man might stride about the platform shouting, waving his arms, and slapping his thighs.

The Athenians never let a citizen become so powerful that he could take complete control of the city-state. The *ekklesia* elected generals, but other officials were chosen by lot, so their appointments were based on pure chance. After a year in office they had to present their accounts publicly,

nized by a council whose 500 members were elected in the various *deme*s, or districts, of the city. Council chairmen, chosen by lot, served for one day each. The remarkable result was that at some time in his life, one in three Athenian citizens found himself, for one proud day, in charge of the city-state.

Many Greeks from other city-states thought that Athens was full of dangerous ideas. They claimed democracy gave power to poor men who were unfit to rule. Athenians, however, were proud of their government. It permitted freedom of speech,

whereupon anybody could take them to court on a charge of misconduct. People scratched the names of any citizens they thought had become too powerful on small pieces of pottery called *ostraka*. On a particular day, these shards were cast into a box in the marketplace. If a total of 6,000 *ostraka* were cast, the person with the most votes against him would be ostracized (forced to leave the city for ten years).

Still, some men did become important leaders. The Athenian leader Pericles (*c.* 495–429 B.C.) was well known for his ability to influence the *ekklesia*. "Persuasion lived on his lips," wrote one Greek poet. "He cast a spell on us."

The meetings of the *ekklesia* were orga-

which encouraged creativity in playwrights and philosophers. And as Pericles said, it allowed the cleverest people to become state officials; what did it matter if they were poor? Rich and poor alike, having a stake in the state, were happy to work, live, and die for it — as they did at Salamis.

This citizen is late for a meeting of the ekklesia. *The slaves, who are part of the Athenian police force, are rounding up latecomers. If they mark the citizen's robes with red dye, he will be fined at the* ekklesia.
Left, above: *A vase painting of an orator making a speech.*
Left, below: Ostraka *with various names scratched on them.*
Above: *A bust of Pericles.*

The Athenian Empire

T he Greek victory at Salamis did not end the wars with Persia. For another year the Greeks fought an army Xerxes left behind, finally defeating these last Persian invaders in 479 B.C.

The following year on the island of Delos, Athens and a number of other city-states formed an alliance called the Delian League and agreed to raid Persian lands, hoping to win back the money spent on the recent war. For the next 30 years the league's forces attacked the Persian Empire.

At the same time, the Athenians began to repair the damage done by the Persians. They rebuilt the walls around Athens and its harbor town, Piraeus. Then they built walls to protect the strip of land linking Piraeus and Athens. When the work was finished, Athens was a strongly fortified city.

Slowly Athens began to dominate the Delian League and the league became the Athenian Empire. Each year the Athenians collected a tribute of ships or money from the member states. In 454 B.C. they moved the league's treasury from Delos to Athens. They pressured the other states to become democracies and to hold important court cases in Athens and eventually they even forced the other states in the league to worship Athene.

The basis of Athenian power is the city's navy and its triremes. If any state fails to pay the tribute, Athens sends a trireme with two officials who demand the payment. When the island of Thasos tries to leave the league in 465 B.C., the Athenians destroy the city's walls, confiscate its navy, and make it pay a large fine. From 463 to 429 B.C., Pericles encourages the Athenians to seek ever greater power.
Left, above: *The Athenian Empire around 450 B.C.*
Left: *An official counts the tribute money, checking it against the amount written down on the wax tablet.*

Art and Architecture

Pericles said that if Athens was to be the center of an empire, it should be a city "worthy of admiration." And starting in 450 B.C. many fine buildings went into construction. Most were temples dedicated to the gods, but the Athenians also built a

large *oideion* (concert hall) and a number of impressive *stoa*s (covered walkways). To finance the construction, Athenians borrowed money from the temple treasuries, which was later repaid out of the tribute taken from the empire's member states.

The Athenians loved beauty. The philosopher Plato thought that the law should only allow the construction of graceful buildings, "so that our young men may drink in good from every side." Public buildings were constructed of local white marble and a reddish rock that was a natural concrete, which builders used for foundations. The finished buildings were decorated with friezes and statues, and then painted in gold, blue, green, and red.

In 447 B.C. the Athenians began to build a magnificent temple dedicated to the goddess Athene. Located on the Acropolis, the hill overlooking all of Athens, this new temple was to be called the Parthenon, and a man named Ictinus was its architect.

Because Greek architects thought arches were unsuitable for large buildings, for this project Ictinus used flat beams supported on columns. He also used several optical illusions to make sure the huge building would appear well proportioned to the observer on the ground. If the long sides of the building had been straight, normal optical illusions would have made them appear to sag, so Ictinus made them curve slightly upward in the middle — the centers are 4.4 inches (11 centimeters) higher than the ends. In the same way, each column becomes thinner toward the top, so that it appears straight and even to someone looking up at it. The columns also lean slightly inward,

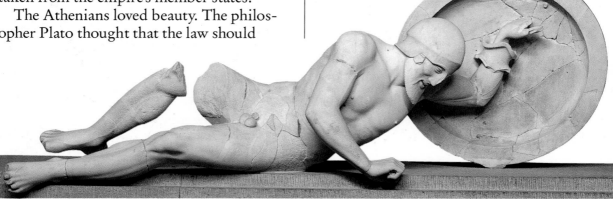

so that the building does not seem top-heavy. The Parthenon took 15 years to complete, and it still stands today.

Below: The Acropolis (meaning "upper city") is the rocky hill overlooking Athens. The largest temple there is the Parthenon. The temple on the left is the Erekhtheion where, every four years during the festival of Panathenaea, the Athenians bring a new robe for Athene's statue. The rest of the Acropolis is covered with temples, altars, statues, memorial stones, and storehouses. The State Treasury of Athens is also here. On a pedestal in front of the wall in the center of the Acropolis stands a huge bronze statue of Athene. Athenian sailors know they are almost home when they see on the horizon the glint of the sun on her helmet and spear.

Far left: Over the centuries Greek sculpture develops greatly. Early Greek figures are known as kouroi *(c. 600 B.C.). Inspired by Egyptian sculptures, they show their subjects standing stiffly, one foot in front of the other.*

Left, below: A century later (c. 490 B.C.) artists create more lifelike statues, like this one of a fallen warrior.

Right: By the first century B.C. Greek sculptors use their understanding of the muscles beneath the skin to achieve an even greater feeling of reality. The sculptor of the resting boxer has signed his name on the boxer's glove. He is an Athenian: Apollonios, son of Nestor.

The Theater

Athenian drama developed from ancient festivals in honor of the god Dionysus. Plays were originally performed and judged at competitions held during two religious festivals, in January and March; men, women, and children all enjoyed going to the open-air theater to see the plays.

The first plays consisted of a single speaker and a chorus of 12 to 15 men who danced and sang to fill out the details of the story. The Athenian writer Aeschylus (c. 525–456 B.C.) had the idea of using a second speaker, or actor. Later writers wrote plays with more characters, but still only three actors were allowed to take part in one play. Each actor had to play a number of parts, wearing a different mask for each character; all female roles were played by men, as acting was considered improper for women. Plays were performed only twice a year in Athens, but actors often

toured Greece during the rest of the year.

The early form of Greek drama was called tragedy; it told stories of the gods, goddesses, and heroes. Later plays were about everyday life and were called comedies. In Athens, where freedom of speech was permitted, the writers of comedies mocked the political leaders of the time, the gods, and even more dangerously, the audience. The comic writer Aristophanes (*c.* 450–388 B.C.) often included a few lines attacking other playwrights.

The plays were very popular; the theater of Dionysus in Athens seated 14,000 people. Nevertheless, audiences threw food and even stones if they disliked a play. One actor had so many figs thrown at him that it was said he could have started a fruit stall.

In a scene from the Oresteia *tragedies by Aeschylus, the hero Agamemnon is trapped in a net by his wife (and her accomplice, Aegisthus) and killed because he has sacrificed one of his daughters to the gods. The actors wear masks and thick-soled shoes so that the audience can see them clearly.*

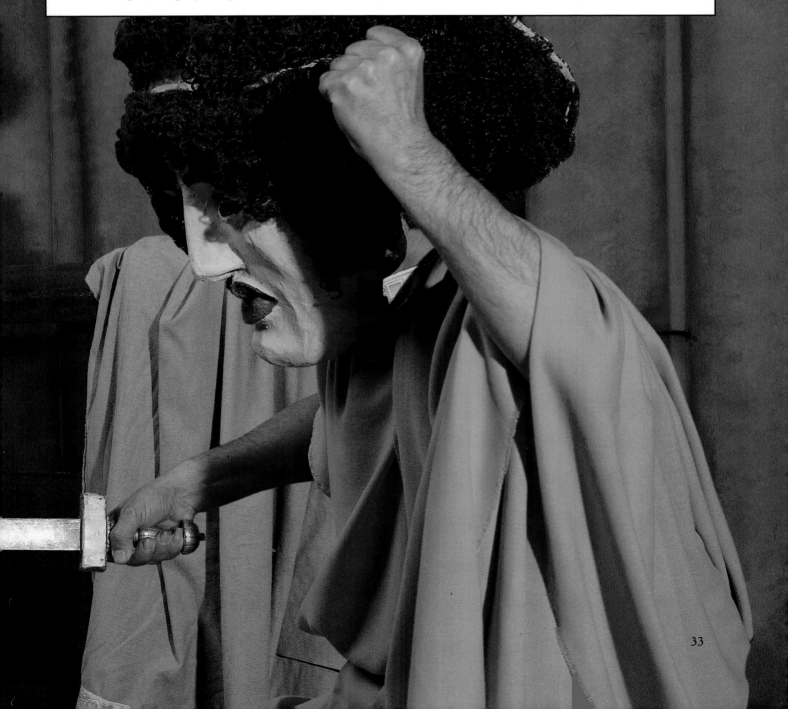

Knowledge and Philosophy

As Greek colonists traveled to different areas of the Mediterranean, they met people with a wide variety of beliefs. Historians think that this exposure to new ideas led them to investigate a number of ways of looking at the world. The Greek word *philosophos* means "a man who likes to be wise," and a philosopher spent his life asking questions; he might study science, art, and morals at the same time — and he didn't always come up with answers.

When the oracle at Delphi told Socrates that he was the wisest man in Greece, Socrates was puzzled; *he* thought he knew very little. In the end he decided that his wisdom lay in the fact that he *knew* that he knew very little and was therefore trying to learn more. "A life lived without asking questions is no life at all," he said.

The Greeks were the first Western people to write books on geography, history, and science. Pythagoras (*c.* 580–500 B.C.) studied mathematics and geometry; his theory about the proportions of right-angled triangles is one of the basics of geometry. Archimedes (*c.* 287–212 B.C.) discovered what is called specific gravity — the weight of the water a body displaces is proportional to the weight of the body itself when he climbed into his bath one day.

Anaximander (*c.* 610–546 B.C.) said that the earth was not flat, as many people thought, but a solid body hanging in space. Other Greek philosophers realized that the world is millions of years old and that fossils are creatures preserved from an earlier age. Several writers even suggested that all matter is composed of tiny atoms too small to be seen. All these ideas, however, were lost during the Middle Ages, and it would be more than 2,000 years before other scientists realized that they are correct.

The Greek philosophers looked for rational (common-sense) answers to their questions. Many doubted the stories generally told about the gods and goddesses. Did the immortals really look like human beings? Probably not, thought the writer Xenophanes (*c.* 560–478 B.C.): "The Ethiopians say that their gods are black. . . . If horses could draw, they would draw their gods looking like horses." Some thinkers doubted whether the gods existed at all.

The Greeks developed concepts of logic and many rules of argument. Modern lawyers still try cases using argument from probability (asking, "Is it likely?"). Above all, the Greeks realized that there are two sides to every question: "Sickness is bad for the sick but good for the doctor; a worn-out shoe is bad for the owner but good for the cobbler." This idea of oppositions became very important in Greek thought.

Greek philosophers loved to struggle with complicated ideas. They liked to deduce truths about specific cases from general laws: *All men are mortal; Socrates is a man; therefore Socrates is mortal.* Another favorite argument uses the same method to jokingly "prove" that your father is a dog: *If a dog has puppies he is a* father, *and if he is* your *dog, he must be* your father.

Philosophy became very fashionable. Aristophanes mocked the fashion for asking questions such as "Why?" and "What?" Even uneducated men, he wrote, had barely arrived home before they started to scream, "Why isn't my jug here? What's the matter? Who's eaten my olives?"

During the time of Pericles, many Greek philosophers went to live in Athens, attracted by the opportunities that democracy and freedom of speech offered there.

Even in Athens, however, ordinary people still believed in the gods and goddesses; to some of these people the philosophers and all their questions seemed dangerous.

Below: Socrates' pupil Plato (c. 427–347 B.C.) opens a school of philosophy in Athens. He uses Socrates' method of teaching, asking his pupils questions rather than giving them information or facts to memorize.
Left: Archimedes in his bath. People still echo his famous cry, "Eureka!" ("I have found it!"), when they make discoveries.

Doctors and Medicine

Starting in the sixth century B.C., many city-states began to establish temple-hospitals. These were called *asklepeia*, after Asklepios, the god of medicine. Patients believed that the god came to cure them during the night; historians now suspect that the doctors drugged their patients, then treated them while they slept.

After about 460 B.C., Greek doctors adopted a complicated theory of healing, based on the idea that all matter was made up of four elements: fire, water, air, and earth. They believed that the body was composed of four humors (liquids):

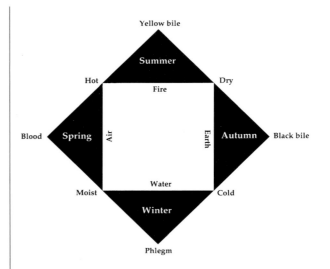

blood, phlegm, yellow bile (vomit), and black bile (excrement). Disease set in if the

humors became unbalanced.

Greek doctors developed a system of natural healing based on controlling the body's humors by the use of opposites. The cure for a cold, for instance, was to keep the patient hot and dry beside a fire. In the hot, dry summer, they suggested, wise people would balance their humors by taking long, cool drinks. In winter they would keep warm by taking brisk walks. Many *asklepeia* became health resorts, with gymnasia, swimming pools, and running tracks.

The Greek doctor Hippocrates (*c.* 460–377 B.C.) developed a system of examination called clinical observation; doctors still use it today, diagnosing illness on the basis of physical symptoms. Hippocrates de-

manded that doctors should be well trained, calm, and caring, "pure and holy in life and practice."

This boy has pains in his arm and side. The doctor examines him carefully. If he thinks the problem is an excess of blood, he will bleed the patient by cutting a vein with a knife or by using the bleeding cup on the table. The cup is heated and placed over a scratch on the patient's back or arm. As the cup cools, it creates a vacuum and sucks the blood out into it.

To the right, an assistant is about to treat another patient for backache by standing on him. A slave brings a flask of urine for the doctor to examine. Around the room are plants and herbs that the doctor prescribes.

Left: *This chart shows the relation of the four elements and the four humors.*

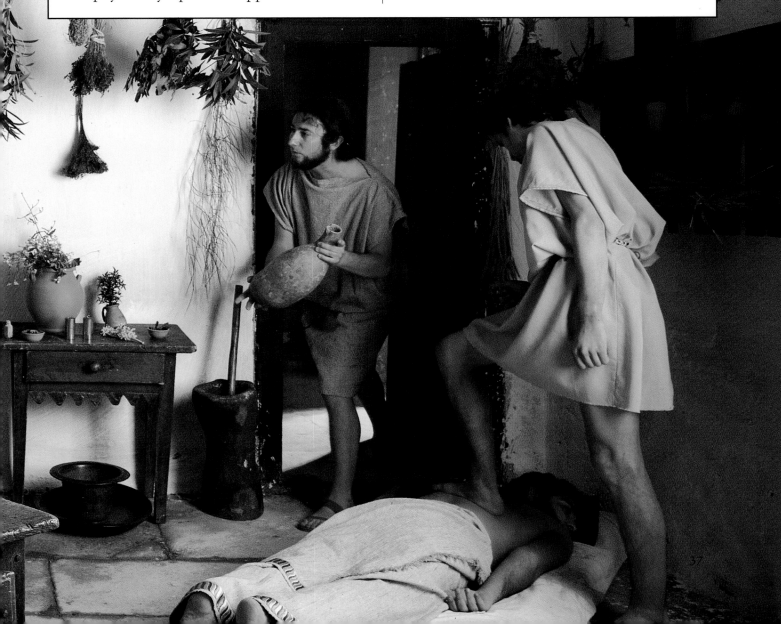

37

From Birth to Manhood

Greek women gave birth at home. In Athens three female neighbors and a midwife would be present. The midwife knew the rituals needed to obtain the help of the birth goddesses such as Hestia, goddess of the hearth — but even a midwife could do little if problems arose with the birth. If progress was slow, she wrapped the mother in a blanket and shook her up and down. Perhaps one in five women died in childbirth. "I would rather fight three times in a battle than give birth once," says Medea, a female character in a Greek play.

When a child was born, the helpers gave a traditional *ololuge* (birth cry). In Athens, most baby boys seem to have been kept and loved, even if they were weak or disabled. If an infant was unwanted, the midwife might arrange an adoption, taking the baby to a mother whose child had died.

Most Greeks would have agreed with the wet-nurse in one play who remarks that "children are brainless things." The Greek word for "infant," *nepios*, also meant "igno-rant." Education was therefore considered to be very important for boys who would later become citizens or, in a *metoikoi* family, merchants. In Athens they went to school at the age of 7, and even poor boys stayed until they were 14. Rich boys continued for four more years, studying astronomy, geometry, geography, history, and rhetoric (public speaking).

At the age of 18 an Athenian boy began two years of military training. When he had completed his training, he offered a sacrifice and was entered on the register of *ekklesia* as a citizen.

Top left to bottom right: *An Athenian pupil learns mathematics, reading, and writing; a slave makes sure that he does not giggle or sit cross-legged. He sings the poems of Homer to learn them by heart. Boys enjoy games such as cockfighting. In more serious moments, boys prepare for the family sacrifice or play the lyre.*

Older boys learn to speak like a **rhetor.** *All pupils train in athletics.*
Right: *An 18-year-old sets off for military training.*

Women in the Family

U nlike their brothers, many Greek girl babies were abandoned. "If you bear a child," wrote a soldier to his wife, "keep it if it is a boy. If it is a girl, cast it out." A census of the inhabitants of Miletus, a Greek city in Asia Minor, in about 220 B.C. recorded 169 boys and only 46 girls.

In general, girls were "given as little food as possible . . . [and] were expected to keep their mouths shut and to attend to their wool." A Greek woman always had to have a *kyrios,* a male guardian; he could be her father or her husband. In a Greek novel written to show husbands how to control their wives, the 15-year-old wife "had lived under the strictest discipline and had been taught to see, hear, or ask as little as possible."

An Athenian girl commonly married at 15; her husband would be nearer 30. The girl's father arranged her marriage and paid the bridegroom a dowry for her upkeep.

Most marriages took place in the month of *Gamelion* (January), the "month of marriages." The bride gave her toys to the Temple of Artemis, Apollo's sister, who was the goddess of virgins and the moon; then she cut her hair, took a ritual bath in holy water, and ate a last meal with her family. Then, at night, her groom and his friends arrived to take her away; her husband carried her over his threshold to show he owned her. There was no ceremony, although the groom's friends sang songs called hymns (after Hymen, the god of marriage). If the marriage went badly, an Athenian girl could obtain a divorce simply by leaving her husband and returning to her father; a man could get a divorce by telling his wife to leave. No reason had to be given.

Top left to bottom right: *A mother encourages her child to use the pot. Another mother bottle-feeds her baby. Women must tidy the house and make offerings to Zeus and Apollo on an altar in the courtyard of their home. One of the few chances they have to meet other women is when they go to fetch water.*

Sending a girl to school is like "giving extra poison to a dangerous snake," says one Greek writer. Instead, Greek girls stay at home and learn the skills they will need to run a household. Young girls are taught to grind corn. Mothers show older girls how to spin and to weave. **Above:** *A bride arriving at her husband's home.*

41

At Home

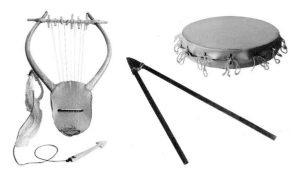

Few Greek men thought women were important: "One man's life is worth thousands of women," says a Greek heroine in a play written by a man. The hero of one of Homer's poems orders his mother to "go back into the house and attend to your weaving and spinning. I will do the talking. For I am the ruler in this household."

"Your business will be to stay indoors and supervise the servants, do the household accounts, make the clothes, and see that the grain is dry," one book advised women. It was considered shameful for a woman to be seen in public, except at a funeral, religious festival, or play.

Poor women had to work, weaving cloth and doing household chores. Wealthy Greek wives, however, spent most of their lives in the *gunaikeion,* the women's rooms. Wealthy men hired chaperones to accompany their wives if they had to go out. A rich woman was supposed to rush to the *gunaikeion* if she met a man who was not a member of her family, even if she was in the courtyard of her own house.

Women and slaves did the routine jobs of society, enabling the men to go to war, take part in politics, and discuss philosophy, but their contributions were not often acknowledged.

In the men's apartment in this house, the husband and his friends enjoy a simple meal. The first course consists of sea urchins with olives, garlic, and radishes. For the main course there is tuna cooked in salt water, with a stuffing of herbs. Greeks like to mix sweet and sour tastes, so the third course is meat flavored with aniseed and cheese. Slaves also serve vegetables, garlic, fruit, and dandelion salad. At the end of the meal, the diners will eat the pastries for which Athens is famous. The men also drink heavily and later they may find they have become drunk.

Educated foreign women, known as hetairai *(companions), are invited, but wives are not. The* hetairai *chat with the men, dance, and play musical instruments such as the lyre,* avlos *(pipe), and tambourine. Later, even these women will be sent away and the men will discuss philosophy.*

Above: *A* hetairai's *instruments.*

Craftsmen and Traders

In Athens trade and crafts were generally left to the *metoikoi*. Some *metoikoi*, like the laborers who waited at Athens's Market Mound to be hired and the tradesmen who sold coal, figs, leather, spoons, books, buns, and seed were poor; but the architects, painters, and sculptors who worked on such projects as the Parthenon and the craftsmen who supplied the warring armies of Greece received good pay.

The Greek philosophers taught that a citizen should devote himself to war, politics, athletics, hunting, and philosophy. Tradesmen, they said, were uneducated and had no time for politics; craftsmen (who worked indoors) were flabby and unhealthy; shopkeepers (who sold goods for profit) were no better than thieves.

This attitude led many Greeks to try to live on the income from their farms. It is ironic that without the craftsmen the wealthy would not have been able to live as they did. "Every skill and invention of mankind is at your service," a commoner tells a character named Rich in one of Aristophanes' plays. "For you one of us sits making shoes. Others work in bronze, wood, and gold. Another washes cloth. Another washes skins."

This pot has been thrown (shaped) on a potter's wheel and lightly baked in a kiln. Now the painter decorates and glazes it, readying it to be refired in the kiln.

Above, left to right: *Greek skill in pottery develops through the centuries. The earliest designs (c. 750 B.C.) consist of patterns and silhouettes; the figures do not overlap. By the sixth century B.C. the vase painters are portraying vivid scenes from the Greek myths, drawing* black-glazed figures on an unglazed red background. *Half a century later they use black glaze for the background and draw details of clothing and muscle on the unglazed red figures. Instead of depicting stories about the gods, they show scenes of everyday life in Greece.*

Slaves

Historians estimate that slaves formed from one-third to two-fifths of the population of Athens in the fourth century B.C. Most slaves were barbarians captured by pirates or soldiers; others were the children of slaves. Some had been abandoned as infants, then rescued and sold by slave traders.

Prices varied from 72 drachmas for an infant to more then 300 drachmas for an educated Syrian man (a drachma was the daily wage of a skilled nonslave worker). One rich Athenian owned 1,000 slaves, whom he hired out at one obol (one-sixth of a drachma) per day.

House slaves did most of the menial tasks and helped the wealthier women to look after children and old people. Other slaves worked alongside the *metoikoi* and poor Athenians on the buildings of the Acropolis or labored in craftsmen's workshops. The city of Athens maintained 300 slaves as its police force, and there were perhaps 40,000 more in the state silver mines, where they worked in terrible conditions.

Some slaves held important positions as clerks, bankers, and ships' captains. If these slaves saved carefully, they could buy their freedom. In the fifth century B.C., a slave named Pasion married his master's widow, took over his master's banking business, and became a citizen of Athens.

Greek philosophers argued about whether slavery was natural or unnatural. The comic writer Crates joked that, however it came about, slavery would come to an end only when cups washed themselves out, food cooked itself, and hot water came straight from the pipes.

In this small shoe workshop the labor is divided. One slave cuts the leather around the foot of the young customer, another stitches the leather, and a third rounds off the shoes. All the work is done by hand; there are no machines. Another slave waits to take the boy home.

In the Agora

In the morning most Athenian citizens who did not have to work went to the agora, an open space in the center of the city. Around the agora stood several temples, the army headquarters, the city records office, a prison, and a public noticeboard listing new laws, forthcoming legal cases, and names of men needed for service in the army. Nearby lay the Royal Stoa, the covered walkway where many of the laws of Athens were carved in stone, and the Painted Stoa, whose walls were covered with murals depicting the city's history.

The law courts were also in the agora. If a citizen thought he had a case against someone, he would go to the Royal Stoa to check the laws, then he would accuse his opponent in court. Court cases started with prayers, then the charge was read. There were no lawyers, so the accuser and the accused spoke for themselves; they had to stop when the water ran out of a water clock. Witnesses were not cross-examined, but crowds interrupted and shouted down unpopular speakers. Evidence from slaves was allowed only if it had been obtained through torture. Jurors, who were chosen at random from a daily crowd of volunteers, acted as both judge and jury. When everyone had spoken, they voted by dropping small cubes into a pot. If the verdict was guilty, punishment was meted out according to a fixed penalty, or else the jury voted again to determine the sentence.

The agora is always full of people discussing politics, hoping to be chosen for jury service, or gathering with their pieces of pottery for an ostracism.

Every day local farmers and craftsmen set up their stalls in the shade of the plane trees here and in the surrounding streets and offer vegetables, fruit, cheese, fish, meat, wine, timber, pottery, hardware, and books to passing customers. Athenians and rural folk alike flock to the agora in search of bargains.

Old Age and Death

There were relatively few old people in Greece. Although some people, such as the philosopher Xenophanes, are reported to have lived to the age of 100, studies of skeletons show that most men died when they were about 44 years old; women, worn out by childbirth, often died even younger, in their mid-thirties.

In Athens men who lived long enough customarily retired at 60. They handed over control of the family's farm to a son. By law the son had to give his aged parents food, a room, and a decent burial. Women were classed as old when they could no longer have children. One benefit of this change of status was that they were allowed to go out alone in public.

The city paid a pension to the parents of men who had died in battle, and to widows who had given birth to male children. Most aged poor people, however, had to look after themselves. Elderly men could earn a little money doing jury service, and women could act as professional mourners at funerals or as midwives and nurses. When slaves became old and sick, they were sometimes thrown out and left to die.

Greeks dreaded old age, with its sickness and senility. Old people were thought

to be "ugly outside and dirty-minded within . . . hateful to young men and despicable to women." Nevertheless, said the playwright Euripides, "it is silly the way old men complain about old age and long life; if death comes close, not one of them wants to die."

A funeral is held on the third day after death. The corpse has been washed, anointed, wrapped in a shroud, and garlanded. It is laid on a bier and carried in procession to a cemetery outside the walls of the city. Sometimes bodies are burned on a pyre. This woman, however, will be buried.
Right: *The woman's grave will be marked with a* stele, *like this one. Nearby graves might be decorated with tall vases, indicating an unmarried person lies there, or plain round columns, marking slaves' graves.*

Far right: *Each year the family will go to the tomb and sprinkle oil on the grave from a* lekythos.

Plague and War

From 459 to 444 B.C. and again from 431 to 404 B.C., there was war between Athens and Sparta. Each wanted to win control of Greek lands and waters. But Sparta could not defeat the Athenian navy; and although the Athenian army was much larger, it could not defeat the Spartan army.

From 430 to 429 B.C. Athens suffered a terrible plague. Many leading men, including Pericles, were victims of the disease. Noblemen complained that tradesmen and merchants, some with no land at all, were coming into the government. Many Athenians lost confidence in their gods: "Prayers and oracles were useless," wrote the historian Thucydides, who witnessed these events. "Corpses lay where they died on top of each other, and the dying lurched around the streets crying for water. . . . Burial rites were ignored."

In 413 and 405 B.C. the Spartans took advantage of Athenian weakness, and the Athenians suffered two disastrous naval defeats. The Spartans entered the city and took over the Athenian empire. But the other Greek states were just as hostile to Spartan rule as they had been toward Athenian dominance. In 371 and 362 B.C. the "invincible" Spartan army was twice defeated by the Thebans.

No city-state could conquer all of Greece. As soon as one state grew stronger, the others united to destroy it. By 355 B.C. the Greeks had fought themselves to a standstill. Then, in 338 B.C., they were confronted with a new military challenger, Philip II, ruler of the kingdom of Macedon that lay to the north. Philip invaded Greece and decisively defeated an army of Thebans and Athenians sent to try and stop him.

The Greeks are no match for the Macedonians. Each Macedonian soldier wears a leather jerkin. His helmet, shield, and greaves (leg armor) are made of bronze. He carries a sword, an 18-foot (5.5 meter) sarissa (pike), and a number of leather pouches (right) in which he keeps his rations, equipment, and stones for his sling.
Below: *Each unit of Greek soldiers fights in a tightly packed group called a phalanx. Here two armies of Greek soldiers confront one another. In the town a woman cries out in grief.*

Philip and Alexander

As king of Macedon, Philip II had total power over his people; the Macedonians believed that he was a descendant of Zeus. Most of his subjects were shepherds with primitive customs; they spoke Greek, but with such a strong accent that most Greeks could not understand them. Philip admired Greek civilization and tried to emulate it. He built new towns and ordered people to move into them. When his son Alexander needed a tutor, Philip hired the Greek philosopher Aristotle. Alexander was later to tell his troops, "My father took you over as nomads and shepherds; he gave you cloaks to wear instead of sheepskins; he made you the inhabitants of cities and gave you good laws and customs."

Philip developed a strong army. He trained his men by sending them on 37-mile (60-kilometer) marches with heavy backpacks. Unlike the Greeks, the Macedonians made great use of cavalry in their warfare; in 338 B.C. Philip made Alexander the commander of his cavalry, getting him ready to rule.

By 337 B.C. Philip's army had gained him a small empire in the Balkans. That year he forced the Greek city-states to join a league, with himself as *hegemon* (leader).

Philip did not rob or enslave the people he conquered; he just required the captured country to help him in his wars. Thus his empire grew quickly.

In 336 B.C. Philip and the Greek League declared war on Persia. Just when the army was ready to march, however, an officer of the court murdered Philip.

After Philip's death the Macedonian army proclaimed Alexander the new king and showed its loyalty by marching between the two halves of a sacrificed dog. Alexander also succeeded his father as *hegemon* of the Greek League. When the city of Thebes revolted, Alexander destroyed the city and sold its inhabitants into slavery.

Then he went to war against the Persian Empire as his father had planned to do.

Alexander and his troops conquered every Persian province they passed through. They set up new cities as they went — at least 16 of which they called Alexandria. In two great battles, at Issus (333 B.C.) and Gaugamela (331 B.C.), Alexander defeated the Persian king, Darius III, whose own bodyguards finally murdered him. When he sat on Darius's throne, Alexander is said to have commented, "So this is what it is like to be an emperor."

Alexander (far left) and Darius (in his chariot, center) at the battle of Issus.

55

Alexander the Great

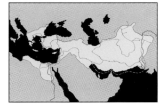

Alexander became the ruler of a vast empire, including parts of Greece, Egypt, Lybia, Asia Minor, Persia, and India. His troops came from every part of his empire; no matter where they were from, the soldiers admired him and willingly called him "Alexander the Great."

Even during Alexander's lifetime legends were growing up about him. Many people — including Alexander himself — thought that so great a man must be a god. One story claimed that Alexander asked an oracle in Egypt, "Am I the son of God?" and was told, "You are." And in 326 B.C., he declared himself to be the son of Zeus.

Some people were not so complimentary. Various stories claimed that Alexander was a drunkard who needed two days' sleep to recover from any drinking bout; that he kept Darius's harem of 365 women, "one for every day of the year"; that he killed a friend who refused to worship him as a god; and that on one occasion he massacred 80,000 Indians.

By 326 B.C., when Alexander's army crossed the Indus River in India, the troops refused to go any farther, and the army turned back. Three years later, when he was 32 years old, Alexander died of a fever in Babylon. On his deathbed he commanded the soldiers to line up and file past him; feebly he raised his head to each one, thanking them for their contributions to his empire.

Alexander's deeds prove that he was a brave and brilliant general who could win victories with very few losses. He was also a genius at organization who, while thousands of miles from home, supplied 100,000 men with provisions and all the materials of war for 11 years. Paying them was not such a problem; we are told that it took 5,000 camels and 20,000 mules to carry the loot from one Persian city alone!

Alexander urging his troops on.
Below: *Alexander, shown attacking one of the Indian army's war elephants, is the first Greek to have his image on a coin — an honor previously reserved for the gods.*
Above: *Alexander's empire in 323 B.C.*

Alexandria

When Alexander died he left no heirs; his generals divided his empire among themselves. Ptolemy, one of Alexander's favorites, took Egypt; Seleucus took Mesopotamia, Persia, Syria, and Asia Minor; and Antigonus claimed Macedon and other parts of Greece.

Where Alexander's armies had conquered, Greek traders had followed setting up small colonies from Egypt to India. Greek became the most common language of the Middle East, and the people of the conquered countries adopted Greek ways. The influence that Greek culture had later came to be known as Hellenism because a Hellene is a Greek person.

Under Ptolemy the Egyptian city of Alexandria became the center of Hellenism. The city, which had half a million inhabitants, had been designed by a young architect named Dinocrates, who had followed the army in the hope of getting some work. Having no success at first, he dressed up in a lion's skin and carried a club; finally Alexander had noticed him and commissioned him to design a great city. Dinocrates laid Alexandria out on a grid pattern, including an agora, a large park planted with plane trees, and a double harbor, with a lighthouse on the offshore island of Pharos.

Ptolemy founded a library at Alexandria, where some of the world's most brilliant scholars eventually held the post of librarian. In addition to producing original works, the librarians copied and edited all the classic Greek poems and plays, and translated famous books written in other languages, such as the Jewish Torah. When Callimachus of Cyrene was librarian, he had all the items in the library catalogued, including about 700,000 scrolls.

Ptolemy also built a museum in Alexandria. This was not a place to keep ancient things but a research center where the Muses (daughters of Zeus who inspired

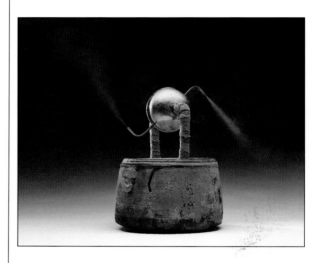

artists, scholars, and scientists) were honored.

Many scientists from Hellenized lands went to Alexandria to further their studies. While the astronomer Hipparchus lived there, he calculated the length of the solar year. Modern scientists using the most sophisticated instruments have discovered that Hipparchus's calculations were off by only 6 minutes and 14 seconds.

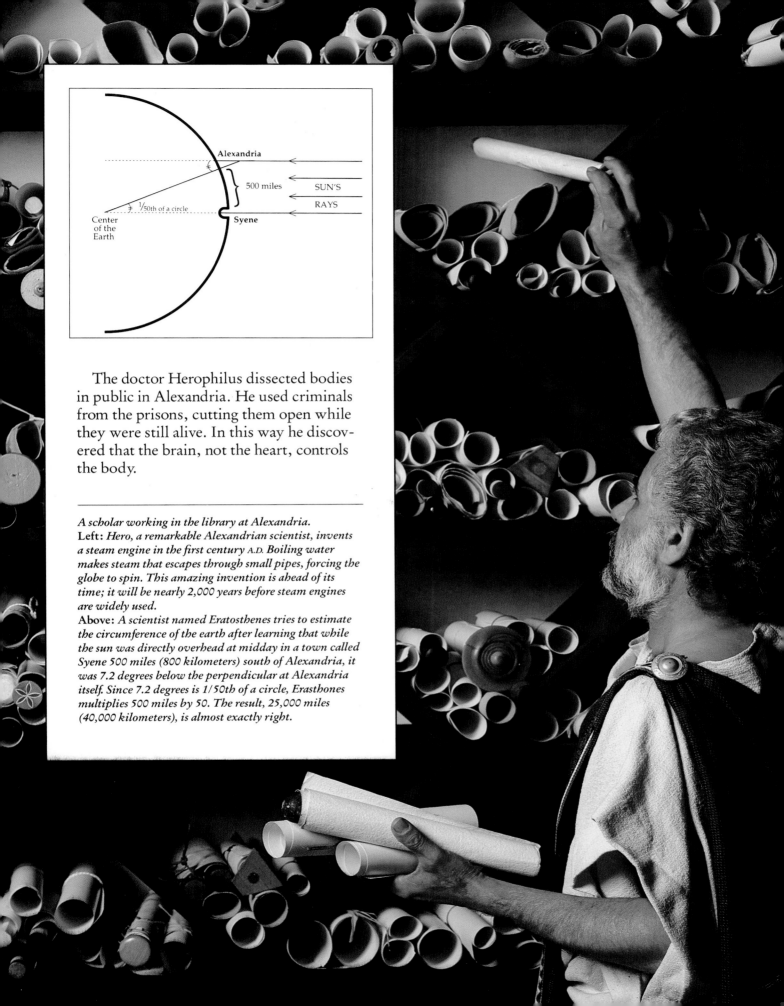

The doctor Herophilus dissected bodies in public in Alexandria. He used criminals from the prisons, cutting them open while they were still alive. In this way he discovered that the brain, not the heart, controls the body.

A scholar working in the library at Alexandria.
Left: *Hero, a remarkable Alexandrian scientist, invents a steam engine in the first century A.D. Boiling water makes steam that escapes through small pipes, forcing the globe to spin. This amazing invention is ahead of its time; it will be nearly 2,000 years before steam engines are widely used.*
Above: *A scientist named Eratosthenes tries to estimate the circumference of the earth after learning that while the sun was directly overhead at midday in a town called Syene 500 miles (800 kilometers) south of Alexandria, it was 7.2 degrees below the perpendicular at Alexandria itself. Since 7.2 degrees is 1/50th of a circle, Erasthones multiplies 500 miles by 50. The result, 25,000 miles (40,000 kilometers), is almost exactly right.*

The Rise of Rome

At the time of Alexander's successes in the Middle East, Rome was a small but aggressive city-state in central Italy. During the next two centuries, however, the Romans grew in power until they surpassed their Greek neighbors. First they conquered the Greek colonies in southern Italy and Sicily. Then, in 168 B.C., they defeated the Macedonians and took 1,000 slaves, including a young historian named Polybius. After accompanying a Roman general on his campaigns, Polybius became convinced that the well-disciplined Roman army could not be beaten.

At first the Greeks were glad to see the Macedonians defeated. In 146 B.C., however, the Romans invaded Greece and destroyed the city of Corinth, carrying off many priceless works of art. Greece itself became a Roman province.

It would seem from their writings that the Romans for their part despised the Greeks. They believed that the Greek Empire had collapsed because the people had become soft and used to luxury. Nevertheless, the Romans admired much about Greek culture; they adopted its architecture, literature, and theater. The emperor Nero attended the Olympic Games, although most Romans preferred their own, more bloodthirsty games. Greek slaves taught the children of wealthy Romans and worked for powerful men as secretaries, doctors, and accountants. "Rome has become a Greek city," complained the Roman writer Juvenal in the first century A.D. "Teacher, speaker, painter, trainer of wrestlers, doctor — these hungry little Greeks know everything!"

This Roman is happily checking the Greek statue his slaves are erecting in his garden while his accountant, a Greek slave, is telling him how much it cost.

"Is there one statue, one picture, that has not been captured and brought here from the places we have defeated in war?" asks the Roman politician Cicero in 70 B.C. Although the Romans have defeated the Greek armies, the Greek way of life has conquered Rome.

How Do We Know?

The Greeks were the first Westerners to systematize the study of history, and most of what we know about Greek history comes directly from the writings of fine Greek historians. The first history books were local chronicles written for Greek colonists. Later the Greek writer Herodotus (c. 484–425 B.C.) wrote an account of the Persian Wars; he was the first person to ask how and why the events of the past had

taken the shape they did (the Greek word *historia* means "enquiry"). Thucydides (c. 460–399 B.C.) further developed the historic method. He chose his sources carefully because he knew that not all sources are equally reliable: "The poets exaggerate; storytellers would rather entertain their readers than tell the truth; even the accounts of eyewitnesses differ according to memory and their own opinions."

The Greeks, who initially borrowed letters from a script used in Syria, were the first civilization in which large numbers of people could read and write. They preserved not only the writings of their philosophers and playwrights but also hundreds of letters written by ordinary people. From these we can learn about family and business life. "If you don't take me to Alexandria, I won't speak to you. . . . I won't hold your hand. . . . I won't eat. So there!" a boy writes to his father. "To my respected father," writes another, "I pray for you daily. . . . May you and my brothers be unharmed and successful for many years. Don't forget our pigeons."

ART AND ARCHAEOLOGY

A man named Pausanias wrote the first travel guide (A.D. 175), describing in great detail the buildings and works of art in Greece, but written material is not the only source on which historians can rely. Although most of the buildings of ancient Greece are in ruins, many have almost miraculously survived.

The most famous ancient Greek building is the Parthenon in Athens. Originally the Temple of Athene, it became a Christian church in A.D. 450 and then a Muslim mosque in 1458. During a war in 1687, when the Parthenon was being used to store gunpowder, a shell hit the building and destroyed its roof.

The Romans stripped Greece of many of its most beautiful pieces of art. Hundreds of years after the Roman conquest, during the 18th and 19th centuries, collectors from all over the world took much of what the Romans had missed. In 1807 Lord Elgin, the British ambassador to the Turks, bought the parts of the Parthenon frieze that had survived and shipped them to England,

where they are known as the "Elgin Marbles" rather than the Parthenon statues. There is still a fierce debate about whether he "stole" the sculptures or "saved" them from further destruction; Greece would like to have them back.

Recent excavations have unearthed many artifacts of day-to-day life. In the agora in Athens, archaeologists have found water clocks, voting ballots from Greek courts, and hundreds of tiny bits of pottery with names scratched on them, used in os-

tracisms. In exceptional cases, archaeology directly supports the written record. The stories of the philosopher Socrates include a description of his visits to the house of Simon the cobbler in Athens. In the southwest corner of the agora archaeologists excavated the ruins of a house in which they found hobnails, eyelets for shoelaces, and the broken base of a club marked with the name Simon.

No Greek paintings have survived, but we have some Roman copies of them, and a great deal of black-and-red Greek pottery. The scenes painted on the pots also give us detailed information about everyday life.

ANCIENT AND MODERN

The Greeks laid the foundations for the modern world by their achievements in pol-

itics, philosophy, science, medicine, history, drama, and architecture. Above all they passed down to us their ideal of *arete* — the desire not only for success and wealth but also for wisdom, justice, and generosity. Speaking in 430 B.C. at the funeral of soldiers killed in the war with Sparta, Pericles reminded the Athenians that these men had died to save the democracy they enjoyed. "Remember that all this was won by courage, a sense of duty, and a feeling of honor," he told the crowd. "Take them as your model, for happiness comes from freedom, and freedom comes from courage." We say similar things today at memorial services for those who have been killed while fighting for their country.

Although you cannot see Greek ideas in the same way that you can see the pyramids of Egypt or the Great Wall of China, they are, in fact, more important. Without them modern civilization would not have developed.

Far left: *A bronze treaty tablet, c. 500 B.C., showing Greek writing.*
Left: *Part of the Parthenon frieze.*
Above left: *A water clock used at Greek trials. When the upper pot was empty, the speaker had to stop talking.*
Above: *A party of French archaeologists who found a* kourous *during excavations in A.D. 1894.*

Index

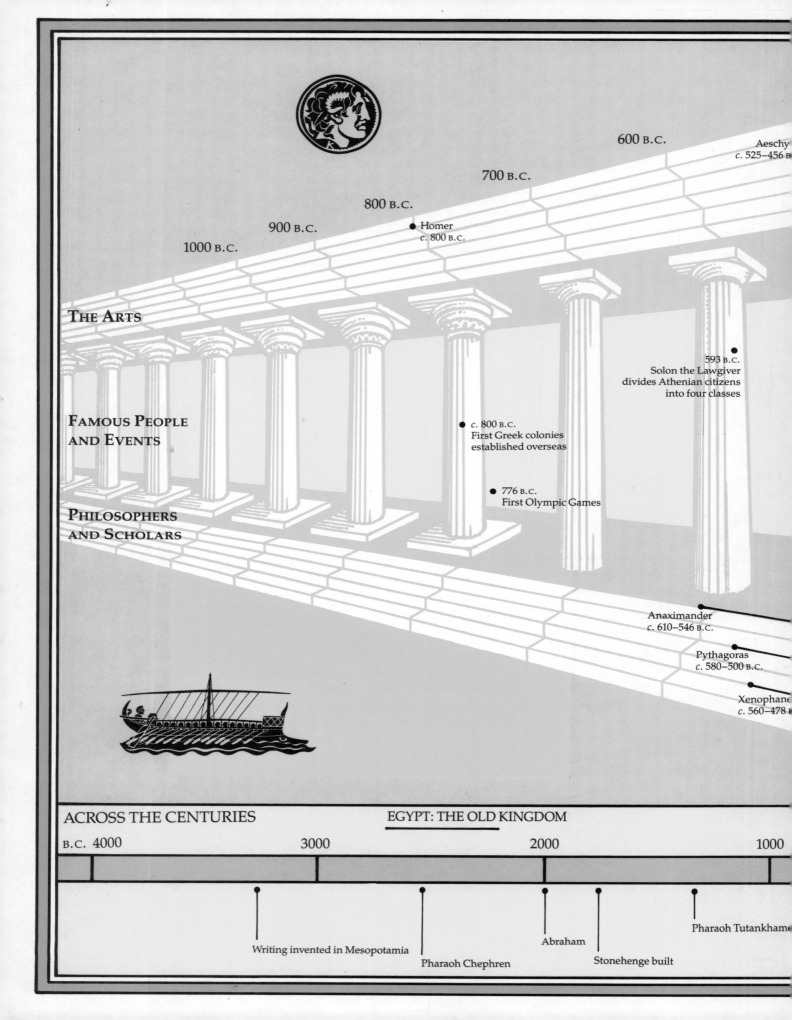

600 B.C.

Aeschy
c. 525–456 B

700 B.C.

800 B.C.

900 B.C.

1000 B.C.

THE ARTS

• Homer
  c. 800 B.C.

593 B.C.
Solon the Lawgiver
divides Athenian citizens
into four classes

FAMOUS PEOPLE
AND EVENTS

• *c.* 800 B.C.
First Greek colonies
established overseas

• 776 B.C.
First Olympic Games

PHILOSOPHERS
AND SCHOLARS

Anaximander
c. 610–546 B.C.

Pythagoras
c. 580–500 B.C.

Xenophane
c. 560–478 B

ACROSS THE CENTURIES

EGYPT: THE OLD KINGDOM

B.C. 4000	3000	2000	1000

Writing invented in Mesopotamia

Pharaoh Chephren

Abraham

Stonehenge built

Pharaoh Tutankhame